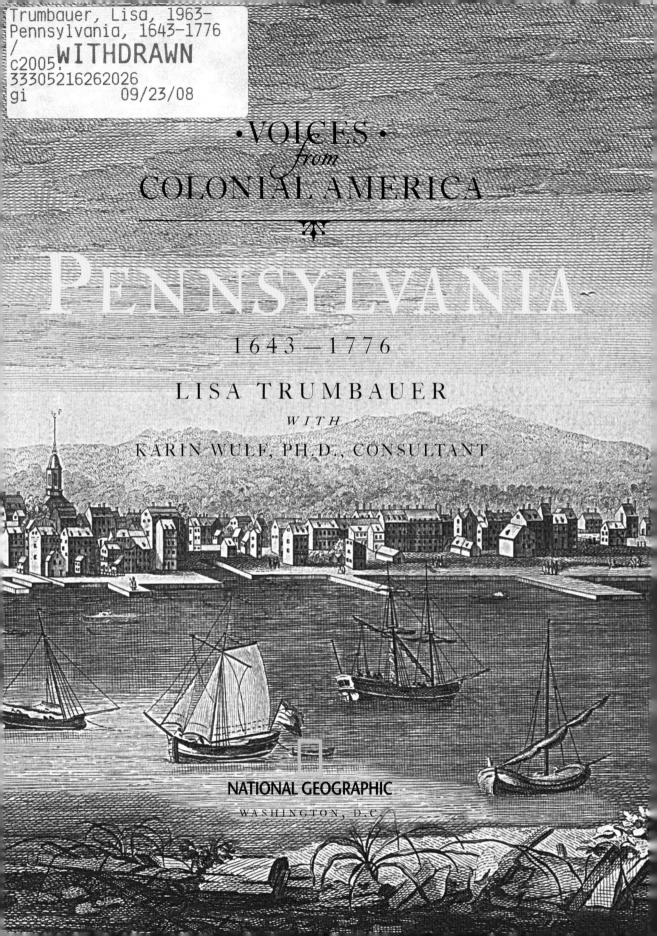

· VOICES ·
from
COLONIAL AMERICA

PENNSYLVANIA ·

1643 – 1776

LISA TRUMBAUER

W I T H

KARIN WULF, PH.D., CONSULTANT

NATIONAL GEOGRAPHIC

WASHINGTON, D.C.

Text copyright © 2005 National Geographic Society
Published by the National Geographic Society.
All rights reserved. Reproduction of the whole or any part of the contents without written permission from the National Geographic Society is strictly prohibited.

John M. Fahey, Jr., *President and Chief Executive Officer*
Gilbert M. Grosvenor, *Chairman of the Board*
Nina D. Hoffman, *Executive Vice President,*
  President of Books and Education Publishing Group
Ericka Markman, *Senior Vice President, President of*
  Children's Books and Education Publishing Group
Stephen Mico, *Senior Vice President and Publisher,*
  Children's Books and Education Publishing Group

STAFF FOR THIS BOOK

Nancy Laties Feresten, *Vice President, Editor-in-Chief*
  of Children's Books
Suzanne Patrick Fonda, *Project Editor*
Robert D. Johnston, Ph.D., *Associate Professor and Director,*
  Teaching of History Program University of Illinois at Chicago,
  Series Editor
Bea Jackson, *Design Director, Children's Books and Education*
  Publishing Group
Jim Hiscott, *Art Director*
Jean Cantu, *Illustrations Specialist*
Carl Mehler, *Director of Maps*
Justin Morrill and Martin S. Walz, *Map Research,*
  Design, and Production
Margery Towery, *Indexer*
R. Gary Colbert, *Production Director*
Lewis R. Bassford, *Production Manager*
Vincent P. Ryan and Maryclare Tracy, *Manufacturing Managers*

Voices from Colonial Pennsylvania was prepared by CREATIVE MEDIA APPLICATIONS, INC.

Lisa Trumbauer, *Writer*
Fabia Wargin Design, Inc., *Design and Production*
Susan Madoff, *Editor*
Matt Levine, *Associate Editor*
Laurie Lieb, *Copyeditor*
Jennifer Bright, *Image Researcher*

Body text is set in Deepdene, sidebars are Caslon 337 Oldstyle, and display text is Cochin Archaic Bold.

LIBRARY OF CONGRESS CATALOGING-IN-PUBLICATION DATA
Trumbauer, Lisa, 1963–
  Voices from colonial America. Pennsylvania, 1643/1776 / by Lisa Trumbauer.
    p. cm.
  Includes bibliographical references and index.
  ISBN 0-7922-6596-3 (Hardcover)
  ISBN 0-7922-6854-7 (Library)
  1. Pennsylvania—History—Colonial period, ca. 1600-1775—Juvenile literature. I. Title: Pennsylvania 1643/1776. II. Title.
  F152.T87 2005
  974.8'02—dc22

                                        2005015798

Printed in Belgium

CONTENTS

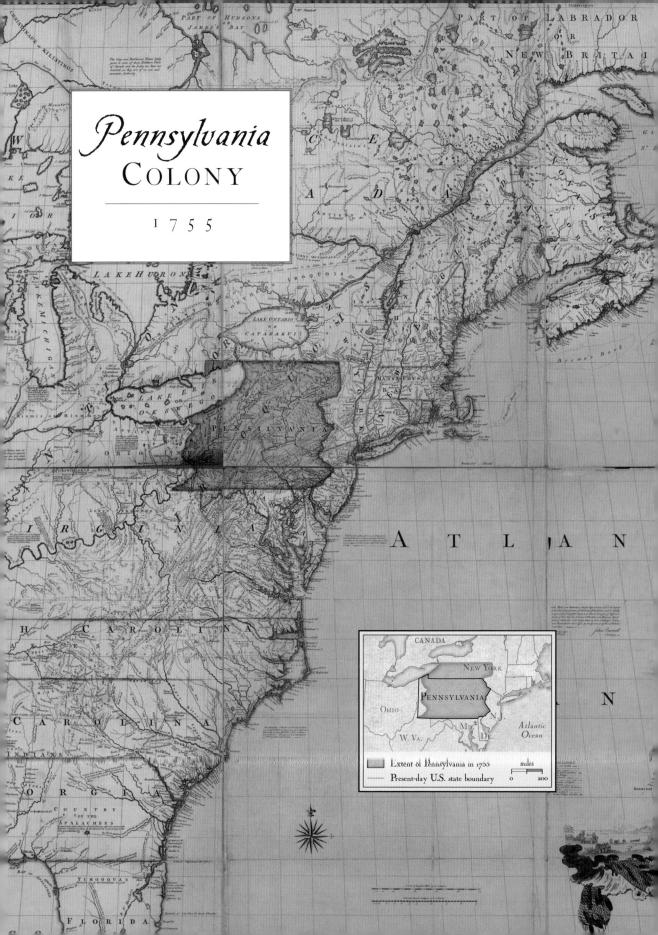

Pennsylvania
COLONY

1755

CANADA

NEW YORK

PENNSYLVANIA

OHIO

W. VA.

MD.

DE.

N.J.

Atlantic
Ocean

Extent of Pennsylvania in 1755

Present-day U.S. state boundary

miles

0   200

INTRODUCTION

by

Karin Wulf, Ph.D.

Colonists eager to support William Penn's "holy experiment" stand along
the shores of the Delaware River. The ship that carried them from
England to the New World is anchored offshore.

The themes prominent in Pennsylvania's early history are still
important today—and may seem very modern to us: racial
and ethnic diversity, religious tolerance, war and peace, and
political experimentation. This volume will help students
understand what is familiar about these issues in our own
time, and what, in fact, is very particular to the colonial era.

OPPOSITE: This historical map, created by John Mitchell in 1755, has been
colorized for this book to emphasize the boundaries of the Pennsylvania
colony. The inset map shows present-day state boundaries for comparison.

Pennsylvania was the creation of one man, William Penn. As the proprietor of this English colony, Penn controlled all the land the king granted to him in a 1681 charter. As a Quaker and because of his intellectual interests, Penn wanted very much to attract Europeans who could share in his vision of a harmonious and tolerant society. Of course they still had to pay Penn for the privilege, and Penn tried to sell as much of his land as possible to settlers to make the colony profitable.

The land that became Pennsylvania, the territory within its acknowledged borders by the end of the colonial period, had been home to many native people, most numerously the Lenape. Other Europeans who eventually settled there, in addition to English and Germans, included Swedes, Dutch, and Scots-Irish. Africans sold as slaves and free people of color also inhabited Pennsylvania.

As the colony grew in population and importance politically and economically (and Philadelphia grew into the largest city in the colonies), these various peoples, with different ideas and values as well as different religions and languages, debated the importance of political liberty and the ethical costs of fighting a war for that freedom. Indians, unhappy with colonial settlers who had pushed them out of traditional territories, ultimately joined with England's European enemies in an unsuccessful but violent effort to regain their land.

JOIN, or DIE.

Benjamin Franklin originally published this cartoon in his newspaper, the *Pennsylvania Gazette*, on May 9, 1754, about two months before the outbreak of the French and Indian War. Franklin was hoping to drum up support from the Colonies to aid the British in their defense of the western borders of America against the French and their Native American allies. Individual colonies are listed in geographical order, beginning with the tail of the snake. Georgia, whose royal charter had not yet been signed by the king, and Delaware, which was governed by Pennsylvania until the end of the Revolutionary War, were excluded. The colonies of Massachusetts, Connecticut, Rhode Island, and New Hampshire are all part of New England (N.E.).

Pennsylvania was an early and eager participant in the revolt against Britain. It may have been the legacy of hot debate and the diversity of its population that accounted for Pennsylvania's first state constitution, which, although it did not last, was the most radically democratic of all the Colonies. The legacy of diversity and the necessity for constant attention to the competing interests and demands of a diverse population are still with us today.

NEW SWEDEN

Sweden was also interested in establishing settlements in North America. The Swedes hoped to start trapping and trading furs. In 1637, Queen Christina sent two ships, the *Kalmar Nyckel* and the *Fogel Grip*, across the Atlantic Ocean. They sailed into Delaware Bay in the spring of 1638.

The Swedes settled along the banks of the Delaware River on lands that would one day become Delaware, New Jersey, and Pennsylvania. This grouping of settlements was called New Sweden. These were the first permanent European settlements in Pennsylvania.

BUILDING A SETTLEMENT

The first ships to arrive in New Sweden brought no more than two dozen men—Swedes, Dutch, Finns (people from Finland), and an African slave, named Antonius, who belonged to one of the passengers. This group of settlers was led by Dutchman Peter Minuit.

Upon reaching the shores of the Delaware River, Minuit and his party did not find evidence of other European settlers. They did, however, meet the Lenni-Lenape, who welcomed Minuit and his men. On March 29, 1638, Minuit signed an agreement with the Lenape sachems, which allowed the settlers to build a settlement on land west

sachem—Native American tribal leaders

of the river, on the site of present-day Wilmington, Delaware. They named their settlement Fort Christina, after Sweden's queen.

The Swedish settlers at Fort Christina felt they needed a safer location upriver, farther from the entrance of Delaware Bay and possible attacks by Dutch-ruled New Netherland. In 1643, the settlers built a new capital on Tinicum Island, not far from present-day Philadelphia. They named the city New Gothenburg, after Gothenburg, Sweden. The governor of New Sweden at Tinicum Island was Johan Printz.

New Sweden was not a resounding success. Many colonists died from disease, and food was scarce. Distrust between the settlers and the Lenape led to strained relations. Because of these problems, New Sweden had trouble attracting settlers. At its height, New Sweden had about 500 settlers, clustered in a small area along the Delaware River.

TIME TO MOVE ON

In 1653, Johan Printz left New Sweden, and Johan Classon Risingh became governor of the colony the following year. He arrived from Sweden with 350 new colonists and a shipload of supplies. By this time, the Dutch had built Fort Kasimier, south of New Gothenburg, in order to defend themselves against the Swedes, if necessary. Nevertheless, Risingh was able to seize the fort and push the Dutch out.

In 1650 much of the area that would become Pennsylvania still belonged
to the Indians. Although the Dutch controlled most of the land between
the Susquehanna and Delaware Rivers, the first successful settlements
were established by the Swedes in New Sweden. The Dutch would win
out over the Swedes in 1655 but would soon face a much bigger problem.
England, anxious to expand its empire along the Atlantic seaboard,
would gain control of New Netherland in 1664.

A thriving fur trade supported the demands of wealthy citizens in New Sweden and in Europe for clothing and accessories like the fur hat worn by the man on the right.

The Dutch were not happy with this new development. Peter Stuyvesant, the leader of the Dutch settlement of New Amsterdam (present-day New York City), sent 700 troops to take back Fort Kasimier and take over Fort Christina. Stuyvesant's retaliation destroyed the already weakened Swedish settlements. The Swedes surrendered to the Dutch in 1655.

The Dutch did not demand that the Swedish settlers leave. They allowed any people who wanted to stay to keep the lands they owned. Only 37 Swedes decided to remain, however, while the rest moved to other colonies, such as Maryland to the south. Even so, the Swedes would continue to be the largest group of European settlers in the region for the next few decades.

During this period, European powers were in steady competition to acquire and control lands in North America, despite the fact that Native Americans were living there. In 1664, England decided that it wanted to consolidate the lands between its colonies of Massachusetts and Maryland. The only thing standing in its way was New Netherland. The English government sent a fleet of warships to America. The ships aimed their cannon at New Amsterdam on the island of Manhattan. Realizing that he could not beat the English warships, Peter Stuyvesant surrendered. England claimed New Netherland as its own. With the area now under English rule, the stage was set for the arrival of William Penn and the founding of Pennsylvania.

CHAPTER TWO

William Penn's Experiment

King Charles II of England gives land to an Englishmen named William Penn, who hopes to establish a colony of peace and tolerance.

ennsylvania was founded by a man with a vision of religious tolerance—William Penn. William Penn believed in a place more understanding of religious and racial differences than that in which he was raised. In Penn's ideal society, *"Any government is free to the people under it . . . where the laws rule and the people are a part to those laws, and more than this is tyranny."*

OPPOSITE: This portrait of William Penn shows the 22-year-old future founder of Pennsylvania dressed in soldier's armor. One year later he became a peace-loving Quaker.

Quakers flocked to the Pennsylvania colony to take advantage of William Penn's promise of religious tolerance. This 19th-century engraving shows a Quaker meeting in Philadelphia. The women (on the left) are separated from the men during the service.

WILLIAM PENN AND RELIGION IN ENGLAND

William Penn was born in England in 1644. At that time, people who lived in England were forced, by law, to worship according to the religion of the Church of England. When Penn was almost twelve years old, his family went to live in Ireland. There, a man named Thomas Loe visited the Penn family. Loe belonged to a

religious group called the Quakers. The Quakers didn't
believe that a person needed organized religion in order to
worship God, nor did people need priests
in order to communicate with God. The
Church of England frowned upon Quaker
ideas and often imprisoned Quakers for
voicing them. Young William Penn, however, was deeply moved by his meeting
with Thomas Loe, who made him rethink his own ideas
about religious worship.

Church of England—
a Protestant faith estab-
lished when the English
Church separated from
the Roman Catholic
Church in the 1500s

As a young man, Penn attended Oxford University in
England. There, he met other people who had religious
beliefs similar to Loe's. With a few of his Oxford class-
mates, Penn began to hold prayer meetings where they practiced Christianity as the Quakers did, without a priest.
Penn also refused to attend services of the Church of
England, because he didn't believe that people should be
forced to worship the way the government said they should.
Consequently, Penn was expelled from Oxford for not
attending the Church of England services.

Penn's father, an admiral in the British Navy, was not
pleased with his son's activities, and for a few years, the
young Penn seemed to put his religious thoughts aside. He
attended law school and returned to Ireland to manage
estates that the family still had there. While in Ireland,
however, Penn once again heard Thomas Loe speak, and his
commitment to the Quaker religion was reaffirmed.

The infamous Tower of London where William Penn was once imprisoned for expressing religious views that went against those of the Church of England

Penn committed his life to spreading the teachings of the Quaker faith. He wrote books and articles on the subject, often landing in jail for going against the orders of England's king. He spent nine months in London's most notorious prison, the Tower of London. He refused to give up his belief in religious freedom, exclaiming, *"My prison shall be my grave before I will budge a jot, for I owe my conscience to no mortal man."*

Penn continued his fight to change people's ideas about religion in England, but he began to feel it was hopeless.

Instead, he looked for a place where people could live with religious tolerance, a place where he could conduct his "holy experiment," as he called it. The King of England, Charles II, had borrowed money from Penn's father. When Admiral Penn died in 1670, the debt had not yet been paid, and the money was now owed to William Penn. Instead of paying back the money, Penn asked if the king would give him lands in the American colonies. Charles agreed, and in 1681 granted Penn 45,000 square miles of land, but only under the condition that the lands be named after Penn's father. Penn didn't like this idea. He was afraid that people would think he had named the lands after himself. Grudgingly he agreed, and the land was named Penn's Woods, or Pennsylvania. Penn looked forward to creating his ideal society and also hoped that this land grant would become a source of great wealth for his family.

holy experiment—William Penn's vision to found a Quaker colony based on religious tolerance and representative government

BUILDING RELATIONSHIPS

Before his arrival in Pennsylvania, Penn sent his cousin William Markham to meet with settlers who already lived on the land—the Swedes, the Dutch, and the Finns. Because the current settlers were from different countries and backgrounds, they had their own ways of practicing religion. Markham carried with him a letter from Penn assuring these settlers that they would continue to live freely, even though England and Penn would now be in charge of the settlement.

Penn's new lands were also home to many Lenape people. He asked Markham to deliver a letter to them, as well. Penn wanted to have a good relationship with these Native Americans, and he vowed that settlers would live only on lands that had been acquired through sales and treaties with the Indians. The letter Penn wrote to the Lenape expressed his intent to do them no harm. He explained through an interpreter that he was aware of the injustices done to them by Europeans in the past.

While still in England, Penn began work planning his colony. He decided to call the capital city Philadelphia, which means "brotherly love" in Greek. Construction of Philadelphia began in 1681 under the direction of William Markham. Penn arrived in Philadelphia on November 8, 1682, and was greeted

MESSAGE *of* PEACE

HERE IS AN EXCERPT FROM Penn's letter to the Lenape.

My friends:

. . . Let me desire you to be kind to them [the colonists] and to . . . receive the presents and tokens which I sent you as a testimony of my good will to you and my resolution to live justly, peaceably, and friendly with you.

I am your loving friend,
William Penn

by both European settlers and the Lenape. A man named John Watson recorded the event:

> The Indians, as well as the whites, had severally prepared the best entertainment the place and circumstances could admit. William Penn made himself endeared to the Indians by his marked condescension and acquiescence in their wishes. He walked with them, sat with them on the ground, and ate with them of their roasted acorns and homony [a dish made from corn].

This famous painting by Quaker artist Benjamin West shows how he imagined what William Penn's meeting with leaders of local Native American tribes would look like. In the painting, Penn extends the hand of friendship to form a treaty between the colonists of Pennsylvania and the Indians.

Shortly after his arrival, Penn officially met with the natives of the area. Along with the Lenape (also known as the Delaware), the Iroquois, the Susquehanna, and the Shawnee also sent representatives. Penn brought several lawmakers to the meeting and spoke with great hope: *The Great Spirit, who made me and you, who rules the heavens and the earth, and who knows the innermost thoughts of men, knows that I and my friends have a hearty desire to live in peace and friendship with you, and to serve you to the utmost of our power. It is not our custom to use hostile weapons against our fellow creatures, for which reason we have come unarmed. Our object is not to do injury, and thus provoke the Great Spirit, but to do good.*

The Native Americans had appointed the Delaware chief, Tamanend, to speak for them. Tamanend honored Penn with a wampum belt. Made of shell beads, the belt which is now on display at the Historical Society of Pennsylvania in Philadelphia, shows two men—a Quaker and an American Indian—holding hands in an act of friendship. Peace between the European settlers and the Native Americans in Pennsylvania would reign for years to come.

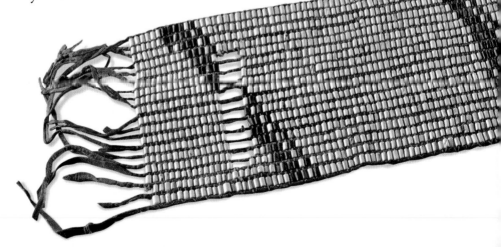

A Capital City— Philadelphia

Philadelphia was one of the first cities in the British colonies that was designed according to a specific plan. Penn had laid out Philadelphia's streets in an organized grid pattern. He hoped this would avoid the crowding he had seen in London, which often led to disease and unstoppable fires. He named the streets after trees, such as Walnut and Chestnut, and imagined stately homes with yards and gardens.

By the summer of 1683, about 80 families lived in Philadelphia. The city would continue to grow throughout colonial times. It would become one of the staging grounds for the American Revolution and play an important role in establishing the United States.

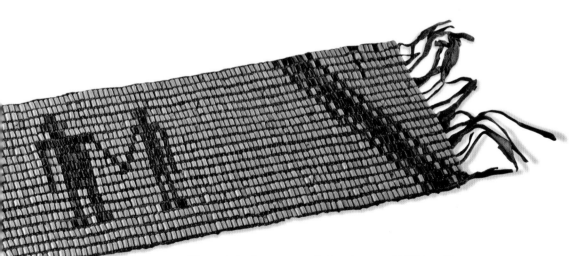

The original wampum belt given to William Penn by the Delaware chief, Tamanend

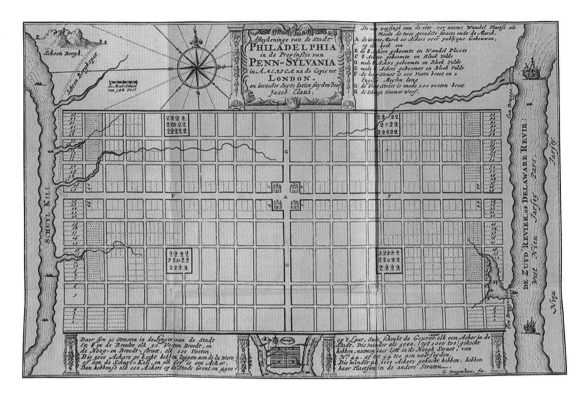

William Penn's plan for the city of Philadelphia is shown on this map,
featuring a grid system that plots the streets and landholdings of early
colonists. The numbers on the map refer to a list of names of landowners.

A MATTER OF GOVERNMENT

William Penn knew he had to develop a government, or set
of laws, for his colony that incorporated his ideas. He knew
that the fate of his colony and of his beliefs lay in his hands:
He wrote, *"these considerations of the weight of government, and the
nice and various opinions about it, made it uneasy to me to think of
publishing the ensuing frame and conditional laws."*

On April 25, 1682, William Penn put into law his Frame of Government, which he had written while still in England. It included 24 points that explained how the government in Pennsylvania would be run. These points outlined the roles of a *"governor and freemen of the said province, in form of a provincial Council and General Assembly, by whom all laws shall be made, officers chosen, and public affairs transacted."* The new law also expressed Penn's desire that the settlers be able to participate in their government. He declared Pennsylvania *"a commonwealth founded on the principle of brotherly love."*

freemen—a term meaning only "free men," excluding indentured servants, Native Americans, slaves, and women

commonwealth—a free state that has a representative government

The house at the corner of Front and Market Streets was the first brick building in Philadelphia. William Penn gave it to his daughter, Letitia.

CHAPTER THREE

Accepting Penn's Invitation

MANY BRITISH, AS WELL AS GERMANS, *immigrate to Pennsylvania to start new lives, but life is not always easy in the Pennsylvania colony.*

Coming to the American colonies and setting up a new life was not easy. The ocean voyage was dangerous, and death and disease were common on the crossing. Yet once the Pennsylvania colony was established, many Europeans, not only Quakers, found their way to it.

OPPOSITE: Known as Penn's Cottage, this house is where William Penn lived during his first trip to Philadelphia in 1682. Although he made only two trips to his colony, he built a large estate called Pennsbury in Bucks County.

ONE FAMILY'S STORY

IN JUNE 1684, JOHN AND JANE CHAPMAN AND THEIR FOUR young children left England aboard the *Shield* to start a new life in America. One of the children, a daughter named Jane, died during the journey. The ship docked in Maryland in August.

While still on board the ship, the family bought 500 acres (200 ha) of land from the ship's captain. The land was in Pennsylvania, north of Philadelphia. The Chapmans are believed to be the first Europeans to settle in the town of Wrightstown in Bucks County. Although the land of Wrightstown had been owned by a variety of people, including a man named Wright, no one had yet built a home here. The Chapmans arrived in Wrightstown in October, but with few supplies and no stores from which to buy materials, they did what many families did at that time— they made a shelter by digging a shallow hole in the side of a hill and covering it with twigs and bark. In the spring, the family built a log house and moved into it.

SETTLERS FROM GERMANY

William Penn's vision of a land where people could worship freely, without persecution from the government, was a vision shared by many throughout Europe. He also, however, wanted his colony to become prosperous, which would ensure his own family's wealth and power. To lure settlers to Pennsylvania, William Penn created pamphlets, which he sent throughout Europe, advertising and inviting people to settle in the colony. Many people accepted Penn's invitation and made the journey across the Atlantic. Large numbers of English Quakers, people of other Protestant faiths, Jews, and Catholics all flocked to Pennsylvania to take advantage of its religious tolerance and economic opportunity.

pamphlets—an unbound booklet of a few pages written on a particular subject

In Germany, a man named Francis Daniel Pastorius was intrigued by Penn's offer of religious freedom in America. He wanted to lead *"a quiet, godly life in a howling wilderness—a heavy task to perform among the bad examples . . . in Europe."* Pastorius bought 15,000 acres (6,000 ha) of Pennsylvania land from Penn in 1682. He hoped to entice other Germans to join him in this new colony. *"Es ist alles nur Wald! [It is all forest],"* he wrote in an article about this new land. Pastorius set aside 5,700 acres (2,280 ha) of the land he purchased for his new settlement, which he called Germantown.

On October 6, 1683, a ship called the *Concord* docked in Philadelphia. On board were 13 families from the German town of Krefeld. These families are historically known as the Original 13—the first 13 German families that settled in Pastorius's Germantown. Pastorius granted each family 3 acres (1.2 ha) of land on which to build a home.

German immigrants would be one of the major European groups to populate Pennsylvania during its early years. By the mid-1700s, a third of Pennsylvania's population was of German ancestry. Mistakenly, they were called the Pennsylvania Dutch. The word "German" in the German language is "Deutsch" (say doytch), which many people mispronounced as "Dutch."

WORKING IN THE COLONIES

People who moved to Pennsylvania at this time were settling in a colony that had an established economy of craftspeople and merchants. Tanners made leather from animal skins, and curriers colored the leather. Rich deposits of iron were discovered in Pennsylvania's mountains, and blacksmiths soon found work making pots, kettles, tools, and horseshoes. Potters created bowls and pots out of clay, and coopers made and repaired barrels in which food and other supplies were stored.

One of the earliest and most important industries in Pennsylvania was papermaking. The first paper mill was built by a German settler named Wilhelm Rittinghausen, or William Rittenhouse. Born in 1644 in Mülheim, Germany, he learned the craft of papermaking in Europe. Making paper is a long, difficult process. In colonial times, it required using old rags made from a fabric called linen.

Linen was made by the weavers of Germantown, who wove the material from fibers of the flax plant. According to a 1692 rhyme:

From linen rags good paper doth derive,
The first trade keeps the second trade alive.

Built on the Monoshone Creek near Germantown, Rittenhouse's mill produced about a thousand sheets of paper a day.

Many colonial women in Pennsylvania worked in the textile industry, carding, spinning, and weaving flax or wool into cloth.

CHILDREN IN THE PENNSYLVANIA COLONY

Pennsylvania did not have a public school system until 1834, so educating children was left to families or the churches. Many families on the frontier owned only one book, the Bible, from which they taught their children to read. Wealthy families might hire a tutor for their children, who, along with reading, writing, and math, learned the classical languages of Latin and Greek.

The Quakers started the first school in Pennsylvania in 1689 in Philadelphia, teaching both Quaker and non-Quaker children. Other religious groups, however, did not feel that children needed to be educated in a school. They felt that learning farming or a trade was more important than "book learning," as described in this couplet:

> Book learning gets the upper hand and work is slow and slack,
> And they that come long after us will find things gone to wrack [ruin]."

Children were expected to help out with farming and other chores around the home. If a family owned a shop in a town, the children worked there, sometimes learning the craft practiced by their parents. For example, if the father was a cobbler—a person who makes shoes—the son might learn this skill. Mothers passed along skills such as sewing, dying fabrics, and preparing foods. Women also might help out in the family shop, making it a true family business. Children understood what was expected of them and how they should contribute to their families as well as their communities.

Children who lived on the frontier or in rural areas worked especially hard helping to run their family's homestead. Sometimes parents had to leave their children for weeks or even months at a time, in order to help out a neighbor, go on a hunting trip, or perhaps venture to a nearby town to sell and buy needed items. A parent might also have to go meet a relative coming from Europe to join the family. A 16-year-old boy named John Reynolds wrote of such a time in his journal:

HORNBOOKS

COLONIAL CHILDREN LEARNED to read with the help of a hornbook. Paper was an expensive item during colonial times. A hornbook was usually made of one sheet of paper containing letters of the alphabet and a religious verse, glued to a small, wooden paddle. In order to protect the paper, the paddle was covered with a very thin, see-through piece of cow's horn. Horns were soaked in cold water for about a month to separate the bony core from the outer layers. The outer part was then heated in boiling water so it could be cut and molded. Pieces of the horn were then cut lengthwise and flattened between heavy plates. At this point, layers of the horn could be peeled apart, cleaned, polished, and trimmed to the size of the paddle.

This spring we planted about an acre of potatoes and a small piece of corn; all the work we did with the hoe. We had no plough, and our oxen strayed . . . In June of this year my father received a letter from my mother telling him that she would meet him at Whiteborough on the Mohawk [River]. . . . My father left me on the 5th day of July. . . . Then began my solitary life. . . . I had not a book, not a scrap of printed paper. . . . Each day I cut a notch on the door cheek, and on Sabbath one of double size. Thus I kept tally of the days and weeks, and often counted the notches to pass the time which hung so heavy. Every night the wolves howled around my cabin, and the owls hooted.

GAMES
Played During Colonial Times

JUST LIKE CHILDREN TODAY, CHILDREN DURING COLONIAL times enjoyed flying kites and playing games. One such game was called jackstones, which is similar to the game of jacks today. Instead of pointed metal jacks, colonial children used small pebbles or even seeds. Instead of bouncing a ball, they tossed a round stone in the air. Children and adults also played a game called quoits, which developed into the game we now call horseshoes.

In this 1745 English print, "The Good Housewife," a colonial woman takes an inventory of household items, including yarn for making clothing and blankets, and bottles probably containing wine or ale.

WOMEN IN THE PENNSYLVANIA COLONY

Some women living in the North American colonies often had more choices than women living in Europe. The Quakers believed in an equal partnership between husband and wife. They also believed that it was all right for women to remain single, which contradicted many other religious attitudes. Many shopkeepers in Philadelphia were women, and several became owners of important retail establishments and taverns.

⨳⨳⨳⨳⨳⨳⨳⨳⨳ PROFILE ⨳⨳⨳⨳⨳⨳⨳⨳⨳

Susannah Wright

Susannah Wright, a Quaker woman who lived in Lancaster County, developed a way to raise silk-worms in Pennsylvania in order to make silk. Knowledgeable in medicine and law as well as a skilled painter and writer, some people think of her as a female Ben Franklin.

Women with strong faith joined a religious community. A single or widowed woman might also make the decision to join a religious community if she faced the prospect of living alone. Living with her "sisters," she would be able to contribute to a group through her own hard work and receive shelter and care in return. At the same time, she could help others by working within the church.

In 1751, a woman named Anna Marie Schemmel Worbass left her homeland of Germany to join a religious community of the Moravian faith in Pennsylvania. In her memoirs, she describes briefly what her life was like:

Towards the end of September we arrived in New York. There
I received permission from Br. [Brother] Nathaniel to go with
Br. and Sr. [Sister] Graff and Br. and Sr. Busse to Bethlehem
[in Pennsylvania]. We arrived there safely on October 6. . . .
On November 3 I moved into the choir house of the Single
Sisters . . . and was happy to have found a little place. . . . On
July 11, 1752 I was received into the Congregation
[officially made a member of the church]. . . . My worldly
business was whatever turned up in the Economy and latterly I
was a cook for the sisters for two years in the Sisters' House.

SLAVES IN THE PENNSYLVANIA COLONY

Pennsylvania was considered a "free" colony, yet many colonists, including William Penn, had African slaves. This was commonplace during the 1700s. Slaves worked on farms and in the iron mines. Many slaves in Philadelphia worked as house servants or in shipyards and on boat docks.

Although slavery was not illegal in Pennsylvania, some people in the colony were deeply opposed to it. One of the very first antislavery meetings in the American colonies was held in Pennsylvania in 1688. It was initiated by German settler Daniel Pastorius. At the meeting, Pastorius made the following comments about slavery:

There is a saying that we shall [do] to all men like as we will be done ourselves; making no difference of what generation, descent or colour they are. And those who steal or [rob] men, and those who buy or purchase them, are they not all alike? Here is liberty of conscience, [which] is right and reasonable; here ought to be liberty of body, except of evil-doers. . . . But to bring men hither, or to rob and sell them against their will, we stand against it.

This engraving shows the Quaker teacher Anthony Benezet (1713–1784) teaching children of slaves in his home. Benezet was hired by the Quaker Friends' English School in Philadelphia in 1742. He was known for his dislike of severe discipline in the classroom and his dedication to providing education to girls and others who did not typically receive it.

Fewer people were enslaved in Pennsylvania than in other colonies. In 1700, a few hundred slaves lived in Pennsylvania. That number grew to a few thousand by mid-century. Beginning in 1758 Quakers wanted their members to free any slaves they owned. Owning slaves implied that Quakers thought these people were inferior. This thinking went against Quaker teachings about equality and brotherhood. In 1780, nearly a hundred years after Pastorius's antislavery speech, the Pennsylvania government passed a law that would end slavery in the colony for good. ※

CHAPTER FOUR

A Prosperous Pennsylvania

*P*ENNSYLVANIA GROWS INTO *a thriving colony.*
Philadelphia becomes one of the most populous—
and important—cities in the colonies.

y the mid-1700s, the colony of Pennsylvania was thriving and robust. New towns and communities blossomed west and north of Philadelphia. Thousands of Europeans looking for a better way of life were lured to the colony.

By 1750, Philadelphia had become the most populous city in the British colonies after Boston. Of Pennsylvania's 120,000 residents, 15,000 of them—more than 12 percent —lived in Philadelphia.

OPPOSITE: This 1788 etching shows the view from Bushongo Tavern, about 80 miles west of Philadelphia. As Philadelphia grew and prospered, new homesteads and towns sprang up in the outlying areas.

A COLONIAL
MELTING POT

PENNSYLVANIA IS SOMETIMES CONSIDERED AMERICA'S first melting pot. Along with the English and the Germans, immigrants to Pennsylvania included Dutch, Swiss, and Scots-Irish—people of Scottish ancestry who had settled in Ireland. Although conflicts did arise between people who came from different backgrounds, for the most part, the settlers accepted their neighbors.

Because of its growing population, Philadelphia became a popular port of entry. Although Philadelphia was not on the Atlantic, it was connected to the ocean by the Delaware River and Delaware Bay. Immigrants from Europe arrived there, and many ships unloaded goods from different places around the world for sale.

Many jobs in the busy port city of Philadelphia revolved around the shipping industry. With so many products coming into Philadelphia, merchants were needed to sell goods to stores, which then sold them to individuals. The flow of visitors to Philadelphia also brought about the need for inns (hotels) and taverns (restaurants) and people to work in them.

Building continued along Philadelphia's streets, too. The most notable construction was the addition of a bell tower on top of the State House. (Today the State House is called Independence Hall.) The Pennsylvania Assembly had ordered a bell for the tower in honor of the 50th anniversary of William Penn's Charter of Privileges (Pennsylvania's constitution). The bell was made in London, and it was hoisted into the tower in 1753. Because of Penn's vision for a place where people could live freely, the bell earned the name Liberty Bell.

"The Arch Street Ferry," painted in 1800 by William Birch, shows the ferry boat that linked the busy port city of Philadelphia with farms across the Delaware River in New Jersey.

Onboard the *Friendship*

INVENTORY LISTS FROM THE SHIP *FRIENDSHIP* SHOW THAT clothing, such as breeches (knee-length pants for men) and petticoats (worn beneath women's skirts), was a major cargo:

Just imported from London, in the . . . Friendship, Captain Walter Stirling, and to be sold by James Burd At his store on Carpenter's wariff [wharf], opposite to William Coleman's, the following goods, viz.

Ozenbrigs [fabric] strip'd [striped] duffelds [fabric], blankets, ruggs, bearskins, broad cloths, womens petticoats of sundry sorts, worsted [fine wool] caps double and single, womens worsted hose, . . . mens searlet [a red dye] knit breeches, . . . womens searlet and cloth coloured short cloaks, mens silk caps, writing paper, Scotch linen, coloured handker-chiefs, . . . Blush and white perfian [Persian] mohair and buttons, coloured threads, Scotch white thread, damask [a type of fabric], . . . mens and womens gloves, silk lace, . . . pins, . . . and a great many other things, too tedious to mention.

— Philadelphia: Printed by B. Franklin, Post-Master, and D. Hall at the New-Printing-Office, near the Market.

BENJAMIN FRANKLIN, PHILADELPHIA'S ADOPTED SON

In 1728, a floundering Philadelphia newspaper called the *Pennsylvania Gazette* was purchased by young Benjamin Franklin. The first install-ment under Franklin's ownership was published in October 1729. It soon became one of the most important papers in Philadelphia and throughout the Colonies.

In his autobiography, which was published in 1791, one year after his death, Franklin described his arrival in Philadelphia when he was seventeen:

A portrait of Benjamin Franklin by Joseph Siffred Duplessis

I walked. . . up the street, which by this time had many clean-dressed people in it, who were all walking the same way. I joined them, and thereby was led into the great meeting-house of the Quakers near the market. . . . I fell fast asleep, and con-tinued so till the meeting broke up, when one was kind enough to rouse me. This was, therefore, the first house I was in, or slept in, in Philadelphia.

Benjamin Franklin left his mark on Philadelphia in many ways. He started one of the first public libraries in the Colonies in 1731. One year later, he began publishing *Poor Richard's Almanack*, written under the name Richard Saunders. This small book, which was published once each year from 1733 to 1758, offered witty sayings, many of which are still used today.

In 1736, Franklin was hired by the Pennsylvania General Assembly as a clerk, and in 1737 the assembly appointed him deputy postmaster of Philadelphia. Franklin suggested ways that the city could improve its streets and their lighting at night. He also established the city's first unit of firefighters. He was elected to the General Assembly by the citizens of Philadelphia in 1750. Franklin would have great impact on Philadelphia and the history of the

Well-Known Sayings from *POOR RICHARD'S ALMANACK*

Do you recognize some of these sayings? They were published by Benjamin Franklin in his *Poor Richard's Almanack*.

Early to bed and early to rise, Makes a man healthy, wealthy and wise.

* * *

Haste makes waste.

* * *

A penny saved is two-pence clear.

(You may know this saying better as "A penny saved is a penny earned.")

Colonies up to and beyond the American Revolution. He acted as a representative for the Pennsylvania colony, traveling to London to represent the interests of the colonists before the government in England. He also spent much of his life working on behalf of Pennsylvania and then the United States from abroad.

A 1790 painting that makes fun of the idea of electricity being used for medical treatment was made after Benjamin Franklin spoke out against the practice in his newspaper.

LIFE ON THE FRONTIER

As more and more settlers arrived in Pennsylvania, Philadelphia and the surrounding areas became crowded with buildings and people. Many immigrants chose to leave the city to live in the outlying areas.

Some religious groups, such as the Amish, wanted to live a more isolated life. They settled in Lancaster, Somerset, and other counties west and south of Philadelphia. The Moravians, a religious group who came from Saxony, a historic region in northern Germany, settled the town of Bethlehem.

Other people who chose to live outside Philadelphia did so for economic reasons. Tradesmen often ventured to outlying towns, which were in need of skilled craftsmen. In a new town, they could set up their own shops and businesses with little or no competition.

Land was also more readily available outside the city. Much of this land was still forested, however, so when a family decided to settle, they had to clear the land themselves. After chopping down trees, they used the timber to build their homes. They planted their own gardens, grew their own vegetables, and hunted wild animals in the forest. Far away from city shops, settlers on the frontier also had to make many everyday items themselves, such as clothing and soap.

To the PUBLICK,

THAT the Stage-Waggons, kept by *John Barnhill*, in *Elm-Street*, in *Philadelphia*, and *John Mercereau*, at the *New-Blazing Star*, near *New-York*, continues their Stages in two Days, from *Powles-Hook Ferry*, opposite *New-York*, to *Philadelphia*; returns from *Philadelphia* to *Powles-Hook* in two Days also; they will endeavour to oblige the Publick by keeping the best of Waggons and sober Drivers, and sets out from *Powles Hook* and *Philadelphia*, on Mondays and Thursdays, punctually at Sunrise, and meet at *Prince Town* the same Nights, to exchange Passengers, and each return the Day after: Those who are kind enough to encourage the Undertaking, are desired to cross *Powles Hook Ferry* the Evenings before, as they must set off early: The Price for each Passenger is *Ten Shillings* to *Prince Town*, and from thence to *Philadelphia*, *Ten Shillings* more, Ferriage free: There will be but two Waggons, but four sets of fresh Horses, so it will be very safe for any Person to send Goods, as there are but two Drivers, they may exchange their Goods without any Mistake. Persons may now go from *New-York* to *Philadelphia*, and back again in five Days, and remain in *Philadelphia* two Nights and one Day to do their Business in: The Public may be assured that this Road is much the shortest, than any other to *Philadelphia*, and regular Stages will be kept by the Publick's obliged humble Servants,

JOHN MERCEREAU, and
JOHN BARNHILL.

In 1767 the *New York Gazette* advertised this stagecoach service between Philadelphia and New York. The trip took almost two full days.

Life on the frontier had its hardships. If the weather did not cooperate, crops would be ruined and families would not have enough food. People could not simply walk to the store to buy supplies and things to eat. Many people who lived in the country died of illnesses because doctors and medicines were not readily available.

Another challenge on the frontier was transportation. Moving goods and people across the vast distances through the wilderness was difficult. Only the barest of roads existed, if at all, and these were rough and bumpy. German settlers began making sturdy wagons, covered with canvas, to handle the terrain. Called the Conestoga wagon after Conestoga Creek near Lancaster, they were America's first version of a covered wagon.

The first three counties in Pennsylvania were Bucks, Chester, and Philadelphia. All three counties came under the leadership of the government in Philadelphia, as set up by William Penn in his Frame of Government. People who lived beyond the boundaries of these counties had to travel to Philadelphia to handle legal matters. These people wanted a government that would be closer to handle their needs more quickly than the one in Philadelphia. In 1728, the citizens of Lancaster and other outlying areas petitioned the government to establish Lancaster as a fourth county. Their petition described some of the problems they faced:

petitioned—when a formal message requesting something is submitted to an authority

To the Honourable Patrick Gordon Esq'r Governor of the Province of Pennsylvania, New Castle Kent and Sussex on Delaware and Council.

. . . by Reason of the Great Distance we live from the County Town Where Elections & Courts are held & publick Offices kept, The arm of Justice is weakened, The benefit of many Good & wholesome Laws almost if not Intirely Lost, & ye person who has Occasion to apply to them put to great and Burdensom Expense, Thieves Vagabonds & Ill people— Boldly infest our parts (Counting themselves beyond the Reach of Law) to the Disturbance of the Peace & very great Damage of the Inhabitants it being almost Impossible to take & Secure Such Villains where Justices & Constables are So thin plac'd.

TROUBLE ON THE HORIZON

Philadelphia and other cities seemed like ideal places to settle for many families and individuals coming to America. The colony was growing and improving. Up until this point in Pennsylvania's history, the colony had had few serious problems. The settlers suffered no major uprisings or conflicts with Native Americans, and the colonists generally got along with each other. All that was about to change, however, as war disrupted the peace within the region.

CHAPTER FIVE

Trouble with the French and Indians

CONFLICTS BETWEEN THE BRITISH *and the French,*
as well as between the colonists and the Delaware,
bring war to Pennsylvania's frontier.

illiam Penn had hoped that the relationship between the colonists and the Native Americans would always remain as harmonious as when he founded the colony. Unfortunately, that fragile peace would begin to crumble, and the failing relationship would contribute to the French and Indian War.

OPPOSITE: Angered by the movement of settlers into territory gained by the British after the French and Indian War, Chief Pontiac (shown here holding a war hatchet) inspired a rebellion that led to the Proclamation of 1763.

THE WALKING PURCHASE

The controversy leading up to the French and Indian War (1754–1763) had been brewing for almost 30 years. As more and more colonists arrived from Europe, the Pennsylvania settlers disregarded Native American claims and began pushing the Lenape off their lands. The Delaware were angered by these developments.

The Delaware believed the treaty they had made with William Penn had been broken. James Logan was the secretary of Penn's oldest son, William Penn, Jr. Explaining the Native American's complaints to William Penn, who was living in England at the time, Logan wrote:

> "When the natives sold their lands, it was understood distinctly, that the white people should not settle or encroach upon their hunting grounds . . . The Indians observed their treaties with fidelity, and their boundaries appear to have been always accurately understood by them. The settlers notwithstanding encroached on the Indian lands beyond this boundary which occasioned great anxiety and uneasiness among the Delawares."

In 1728, Native Americans met with colonial leaders in Philadelphia to try to resolve these land disputes. Sassoonan was a leader of the Delaware. James Logan explained that Sassoonan *was troubled to see Christians settle on lands that the Indians had never been paid for* and *that his children* may wonder to see all their father's lands gone from them without his receiving anything for them."

Sassoonan's concerns were justified, but nothing was done to solve the problem. Relations between the Delaware and the settlers continued to worsen. In 1737, the Delaware consented to a revision of their original land agreement with William Penn. In this revised agreement, known historically as the "Walking Purchase," the Indians agreed to sell to the colony of Pennsylvania the amount of land that a man could walk in a day and a half. However, the colonists abused the goodwill of the Delaware's offer. Instead of one man walking, the colonists had three men run across the land. As one man tired and dropped out of the walking purchase, the others continued. Consequently, more land was granted to the colonists than the Delaware had wanted to give. In total, the colonists took from the Delaware 75,000 acres (30,000 ha) of rich, abundant hunting grounds— lands necessary for the Delaware's survival.

The Delaware knew they had been cheated by the walking treaty. Chief Lappawinsoe (above) said that the white men *"should have walkt along by the River Delaware . . . not have kept up the Run, Run all day."*

TROUBLES IN THE WEST

Troubles between the colonists and the Delaware continued to erode their one-time good relationship. Settlers pushed the tribes farther and farther west. Native Americans became hostile toward the settlers, sometimes attacking homes and farms. Colonists began to view the Native Americans as fierce enemies. Every once in a while, the colonial government tried to stop people from moving onto Native American lands, but these actions had little results.

Unrest was also growing in the west, beyond the Appalachian Mountains. Along with the British, the French had established colonies in North America. Most of the French colonies lay either north of the British colonies, in land that today is Canada, or west, in the vast Louisiana territory. The French

NOT ENOUGH
to Make a Change

To prove to the Native Americans that the government had heard their complaints, local colonial forces decided to evict a group of Scots-Irish settlers in the Tuscarora Mountains in Fulton County. Burning the settlers' cabins, the soldiers forced the Scots-Irish immigrants to leave the area so that the Native Americans could live there once more. The town of Burnt Cabins was named after this incident.

traveled between Canada and Louisiana along the Ohio River. Part of their route along the Ohio passed through western Pennsylvania and lands claimed by the British as part of the Virginia colony. Along this route, the French had built forts through the western area of Virginia, Pennslyvania, and New York.

The British governor of the Virginia colony, Robert Dinwiddie, wanted to rid the Ohio Valley of the French presence. Dinwiddie asked a young major in the Virginia militia to meet with the French to express the governor's demands that they leave the area. The major's name was George Washington.

The French refused to leave. Washington reported the bad news to the governor and suggested that the Virginia colony build its own fort. In the spring of 1754, construction began. The new fort was located where the Ohio, Allegheny, and Monongahela Rivers meet.

As Washington was traveling to the site, he learned that French troops had driven British colonists from the settlement, built their own fort, and named it Fort Duquesne. Washington continued on to Fort Duquesne, but along the way, near present-day Uniontown, he came across some French troops. Washington planned a surprise attack in the early morning hours of May 28, 1754. Although Washington defeated the French in this initial encounter, he realized the likelihood of another French attack was strong. He and his troops hastily built Fort

Necessity near Great Meadows. On July 3, the attack Washington had anticipated came. Known historically as the Battle of Great Meadows, it was a victory for the French and the beginning of the French and Indian War.

Washington surrendered and withdrew his troops, leaving the French in control of the entire region of the Ohio Valley.

Fort Duquesne was prized by both the British and the French for its strategic location at the junction of the Ohio, Allegheny, and Monongahela Rivers. This engraving shows British troops taking possession of the fort in October 1758 after it had been evacuated and burned by retreating French troops.

Britain was not about to let the French defeat its army and take over British lands. The French and Indian War would last until 1763, pitting the British against the French in a struggle not only for the lands of the Ohio Valley, but for the right to control North America. Although some Native Americans fought alongside the British, many more sided with the French, including members of the Shawnee, the Seneca, and the Delaware tribes. The French, after all, were more interested in trading with the Native Americans than in taking their land. Hoping to save whatever lands they had left, many Indians agreed to fight with France against the British.

FORT DUQUESNE

FORT DUQUESNE REMAINED in French hands until late in 1758 when the British retook the site. The British renamed it Fort Pitt in honor of the prime minister of England at the time. Settlement began in 1760 in what would become the city of Pittsburgh.

THE STORY OF MARY JEMISON

Life on the Pennsylvania frontier during the 1750s and 1760s was not easy. Settlers were caught in the middle of the conflict between the British and the French.

In 1742, the Jemisons came to Pennsylvania from Ireland and settled along Marsh Creek, in what today is the town of Chambersburg, about 150 miles (240 km) west of Philadelphia. One morning in April 1758, the family was attacked by four Frenchmen and six Shawnee. The mother, father, and three of the four children were killed and scalped. For some reason, the Shawnee and the French decided to spare the life of 16-year-old Mary Jemison.

The attackers took Mary to Fort Duquesne. Two Native American women from the Seneca tribe decided to "adopt" her to replace a brother they had lost during the war. They brought her to their village near Fort Duquesne and renamed her Dickewamis. Years later, Jemison described her arrival in the village:

> *Having made fast to the shore, the Squaws left me in the canoe while they went to their wigwam or house in the town, and returned with a suit of Indian clothing, all new, and very clean and nice. . . . [They] then washed me clean and dressed me in the new suit they had just brought, in complete Indian style; and then led me home and seated me in the center of their wigwam. . . . I was made welcome amongst them as a sister to the two Squaws before mentioned, and was called Dickewamis.*

Jemison married a member of the Delaware tribe and eventually moved north to an area called Genesee Valley in the New York colony. Even after her husband died, she chose to remain with the Native Americans. She married a member of the Seneca tribe, and she and her new husband moved to lands near Buffalo, New York. In 1823, she told her story to an interviewer, and her account was published the next year. Mary Jemison lived to be 91 years old. She died in 1833.

TREATIES AND ROYAL PROCLAMATIONS

In February 1763, the Treaty of Paris was signed, officially ending the French and Indian War. The treaty gave Britain control of French lands on the mainland of North America, expanding Britain's power.

The Native Americans, of course, were not happy with the treaty. They feared it would encourage colonists to move westward and settle on their lands. Led by an Ottawa chief named Pontiac, the Indians decided to fight their own battle against the British, capturing several British forts. The Battle of Bushy Run was fought near Greensburg, Pennsylvania, in August 1763. Chief Pontiac was defeated, and the British were finally able to put down their weapons. After several meetings with the Indians to discuss a peace, the British government eventually decreed that the colonists had been unjust toward the Indians. Britain's king, George III, declared a Royal Proclamation on October 7, 1763. It established a boundary between the Colonies and Indian lands. White settlers were now prohibited from moving into lands west of the Appalachians. In his proclamation, the King stated:

And whereas great Frauds and Abuses have been committed in the purchasing Lands of the Indians . . . We do . . . strictly enjoin and require, that no private person do presume to make any Purchase from the said Indians of any lands reserved to the said Indians within those Parts of our Colonies where we have thought proper to allow settlement.

Not all colonists agreed with or found comfort in the king's proclamation. A group of more than a hundred Pennsylvania men called the Paxton Boys decided they wanted to rid the Pennsylvania colony completely of Native Americans. In December 1763, the Paxton boys killed 20 members of the peaceful Susquehannock tribe who resided in a small village at Conestoga in the Lancaster area. The Paxton Boys then set out to kill about a hundred Native Americans who had taken refuge in Pennsylvania. Benjamin Franklin convinced the violent group of colonists to cease their activities.

proclamation—a formal public statement

The Paxton Boys were never punished or held responsible for their actions. Many colonists were skeptical about the king's reasons for protecting the Indians. This distrust would become a significant factor as Great Britain sought the Colonies' help in recovering from the French and Indian War.

Its victory in the war had left Great Britain in debt. To cover the expenses of the war, Parliament, Britain's law-making body, decided to tax the colonists. These taxes would soon become the catalyst for another war—the American Revolution. ※

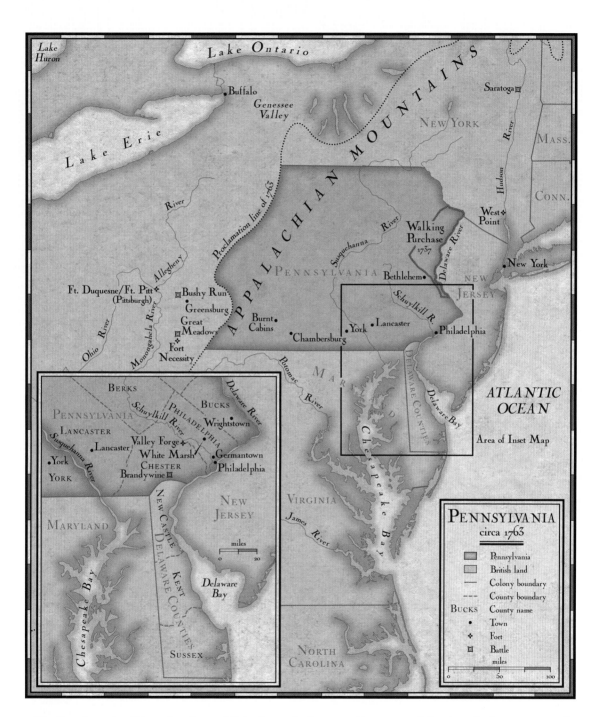

The Proclamation Line of 1763 prohibited people from settling west of the Appalachians. Most of Pennsylvania's population lived in Philadelphia and surrounding counties. The Delaware Counties, which were governed by Pennsylvania, gave the colony vital trade access to the Atlantic Ocean.

CHAPTER SIX

Revolution Is in the Air

UNHAPPY WITH BRITISH RULE, *colonists discuss independence, sending delegates to Philadelphia to the First Continental Congress.*

D uring the French and Indian War, Britain had spent money in the Colonies to protect their territorial claims. Britain also had to secure its holdings in North America against possible future attacks by France. As a result, the British government was heavily in debt. Political infighting between those loyal to Britain and those wanting independence, and financial hardship caused by new taxes in the Colonies were an explosive mix that would set the stage for rebellion.

OPPOSITE: Word that the Paxton Boys were planning to march on Philadelphia to force the government to order the extermination of all Indians in the region caused great concern in the city. This 1764 cartoon by Henry Dawkins shows the militia assembled in front of the Old Court House, guns at the ready.

This engraving of Quakers in Philadelphia shows their practice of dressing plainly. They believed spending money on the latest fashions was wasteful and vain.

PENNSYLVANIA'S OWN GOVERNMENT

William Penn's first Frame of Government had outlined a government with two governing bodies—the Council and the Assembly—and a leader, the governor. William Penn was Pennsylvania's first governor. The Council proposed laws and made sure the laws were followed after they were approved. The Assembly discussed the Council's suggested laws and voted on whether the proposed measures should become laws, but it had no authority to propose laws for Pennsylvania.

Men who belonged to the Assembly wanted that right. In 1696, William Markham, acting as governor on behalf of William Penn, ended the conflict between the two governing bodies by allowing both the Council and the Assembly to propose laws. In 1699, William Penn returned to Pennsylvania to set up the Charter of Privileges, which expanded the rights of freemen. It would continue to be Pennsylvania's system of government until 1776.

One of the biggest challenges facing the Pennsylvania government was the citizens' opposing views on war and violence among its people. The Quakers did not believe in violence or in wars, and many of the men in the Pennsylvania legislature were Quakers. As noted by Ben Franklin in his autobiography, "*My being many years in the Assembly, the majority of which were constantly Quakers, gave me frequent opportunities of seeing the embarrassment given them by their principle against war . . . by order of the crown [the King of England and the English government], to grant aids for military purposes.*"

The violent battles of the French and Indian War greatly troubled all Quakers, including those in the Pennsylvania government. Quakers and other pacifists did not have to

pacifists—people who oppose the use of force to settle disagreements

serve in the army because of their religious beliefs. Slowly, as many Quakers resigned from the Pennsylvania legislature in protest of the colony's participation in the war, members of other religious groups began to have a greater voice in Pennsylvania politics.

Quaker Peace Testimony

A HUNDRED YEARS BEFORE THE FRENCH AND INDIAN WAR, Quakers in England had announced that they believed in peace and nonviolence. However, because the Quakers would not join the English military, they felt they had to assure the government that they would not take up arms *against* England. So in 1660 one of the founders of the Quaker faith, George Fox, presented a declaration of peace to the King of England.

A declaration from the harmless and innocent people of God, called Quakers, against all sedition [acts against the government], plotters, and fighters in the world: For removing the ground of jealousy and suspicion from magistrates and people concerning wars and fightings.

The declaration was a guarantee from the Quakers that they would not fight against the government.

New Taxes

In the 1760s, Britain began taxing the colonists on such everyday items as paper, tea, and sugar that the colonists imported from Britain.

The colonists thought that since they had their own government in the colony but no representative in the British government, Parliament had no right to tax them. Doing so was "taxation without representation," which the enraged colonists felt was unjust. Soon the colonists began boycotting—or refusing to use—items imported from Britain. They chose to use goods they made themselves, such as fabrics they had woven and paper manufactured in the Colonies. Instead of drinking tea imported from Britain, they bought tea from the Dutch, even though it was more expensive.

Patriots, angry with Britain's Parliament for imposing unfair taxes and laws on the Colonies, prepare to string up and burn a straw-stuffed dummy of a representative of the king.

THE FEMALE PATRIOTS

The poem, "The female Patriots," was written by a Pennsylvania woman named Hannah Griffitts in 1768. The poem expresses a woman's point of view about the problems between the colonists and the British government. The poem refers to taxed items, such as tea and paper, and how the women propose that the colonists use "homespun" products from Pennsylvania. (Note that the word Sylvania refers to Pennsylvania.)

Rather than take up arms, most women supported the Patriot cause by using homemade goods rather than buying imported British products.

Since the Men from a Party, or fear
   of a Frown,
Are kept by a Sugar-Plumb [fairy,] quietly down.
Supinely asleep, & depriv'd of their Sight
Are strip'd of their Freedom, & rob'd of their Right.
If the Sons [Patritots] (so degenerate)
the Blessing [the right of power] despise,
Let the Daughters of Liberty, nobly arise,
And tho' we've no Voice, but a negative here
The use of the Taxables [things that are taxed], let us forebear,
(Then Merchants import till yr. [your] Stores are all full
May the Buyers be few & yr. Traffick be dull.)

Stand firmly resolved & bid Grenville [Britain's
   prime minister] to see
That rather than Freedom, we'll part with our Tea
And well as we love the dear Draught [tea] when a dry,
As American Patriots,—our Taste we deny,
Sylvania's gay Meadows, can richly afford,
To pamper our Fancy, or furnish our Board [food and drink],
And Paper sufficient (at home) still we have,
To assure the Wise-acre [jokester], we will not sign Slave.
When this Homespun shall fail, to remonstrate our Grief
We can speak with the Tongue or scratch [write] on a Leaf.
Refuse all their Colours, tho richest of Dye,
The juice of a Berry—our Paint can supply,
To humour our Fancy—& as for our Houses,
They'll do without painting as well as our Spouses,
While to keep out the Cold of a keen winter Morn
We can screen the Northwest, with a well polish'd Horn,
And trust me a Woman by honest Invention
Might give this State [Doctor] a Dose of Prevention [drink of tea].
Join mutual in this, & but small as it seems
We may Jostle a Grenville & puzzle his Schemes
But a motive more worthy our patriot Pen,
Thus acting—we point out their Duty to Men,
And should the bound Pensioners [politicians], tell us to hush
We can throw back the Satire by biding them blush.

THE FIRST CONTINENTAL CONGRESS

In the fall of 1774, 56 delegates from all the 13 Colonies except Georgia met in Philadelphia's Carpenters' Hall to talk about the problems the colonists faced with Britain. Known as the First Continental Congress, this gathering of delegates met for about six weeks, from September 5 to October 26, and succeeded in drawing up a Declaration of Rights. This document, addressed to the King of England, asked that the British treat the colonists more fairly and stated that Parliament had no right to tax them without their consent. The petition was signed by the delegates, including Samuel Adams, Thomas Jefferson, Patrick Henry, John Hancock, and Ben Franklin.

The British government rejected the declaration of the First Continental Congress and, fearing unrest, sent troops to Massachusetts. In April

An oil painting by Clyde O. Deland shows members of the First Continental Congress as they assemble in front of Carpenters' Hall in Philadelphia in 1774. Shown left to right are George Washington, Patrick Henry, and Richard Henry Lee— three delegates from Virginia.

1775, British troops marched to the town of Lexington with orders to seize gunpowder stockpiled by the colonial militia. About 70 untrained American men, armed with rifles, met the British soldiers. The British commander told the colonists to drop their weapons. No one is sure who shot first, but when the fight was over, eight colonists had been killed. This battle marked the beginning of the Revolutionary War.

THE SECOND CONTINENTAL CONGRESS

In May 1775, the Second Continental Congress met in Philadelphia to discuss how to repair the Colonies' relationship with Britain and prevent further bloodshed. On July 8, 1775, a petition was sent to Britain, asking that peace be restored. Written by John Dickinson of Pennsylvania, it was called the Olive Branch Petition. (An olive branch is a traditional symbol of peace and goodwill.) It described the colonists as *"[his] Majesty's faithful subjects"* and it explained that the delegates of the Continental Congress hoped *"to use all the means in our power . . . for stopping the further [spill] of blood, and for [preventing] the impending [disasters] that threaten the British Empire."*

King George did not accept the colonists' olive branch. He had had enough of the rebellious colonists, and he ordered the British troops to use more force to stop the rebellion. The Americans and the British were officially at war.

DECLARING INDEPENDENCE

In January 1776, Thomas Paine, an Englishman who had moved to Philadelphia in 1774, wrote "Common Sense." He presented clear arguments for independence from Britain. Though many in Pennsylvania still respected the king, and others hoped that war would not be necessary, and still others disagreed that independence should be the colonists' goal, enough people became convinced by writers such as Paine that independence was the only possible path.

When the Continental Congress met in June 1776, Richard Henry Lee from Virginia stood up and declared that *"these United Colonies are, and of right ought to be, free and independent States; that they are absolved from all allegiance to the British Crown; and that all political connection between them and the State of Great Britain is, and ought to be, totally dissolved."*

Pennsylvania's Signers of the DECLARATION OF INDEPENDENCE

ON AUGUST 2, 1776 NINE men from Pennsylvania signed the Declaration of Independence:

GEORGE CLYMER, supplier of food and gunpowder during the American Revolution

BENJAMIN FRANKLIN, writer, inventor, and diplomat

ROBERT MORRIS, fundraiser for the American Revolution

JOHN MORTON, lawyer and judge

GEORGE ROSS, lawyer

BENJAMIN RUSH, doctor

JAMES SMITH, lawyer

GEORGE TAYLOR, owner of an iron foundry

JAMES WILSON, lawyer and writer

It was very important that Pennsylvania agree to support independence. If Pennsylvania sided with the British, then the country would be geographically divided. Pennsylvania became the keystone of the rebellion, a state that sat firmly between the northern states and the southern states, holding the country together. (Keystone State is Pennsylvania's nickname.)

keystone—an architechural term describing the central supporting element that holds a structure in place

The decision for Pennsylvania lay in the hands of John Morton, one of Pennsylvania's seven delegates. Morton was deeply torn, but in the end, he was Pennsylvania's deciding vote for independence. The Declaration of Independence, the formal document officially declaring the United States of America's independence from Great Britain, was adopted on July 4, 1776.

CHAPTER SEVEN

War!

As the capital of the Colonies, *Philadelphia is a primary target of the British. Fighting fatigue and starvation, the Continental Army tries to survive a winter at Valley Forge.*

 he opening paragraphs of the Declaration of Independence condemned the British government for not honoring the colonists' basic human rights—the right to "life, liberty, and the pursuit of happiness." The Declaration also established that the governed (people ruled by a government) have the right to dissolve a government if it does not protect the rights of its people.

These paragraphs also officially stated America's intention to separate and "dissolve political bands" with Britain. It was the only choice the colonists felt they had left. The only way to obtain that independence was through war.

OPPOSITE: The Declaration of Independence was first read in public on July 8, 1776, in the State House Yard in Philadelphia.

General George Washington, Commander-in-Chief
of the Continental Army

THE CONTINENTAL ARMY

The American Army that fought during the Revolutionary War under the leadership of General George Washington was called the Continental Army. The British troops in America were led by General Sir William Howe.

The British Army had many advantages over the Continental Army. British soldiers were well equipped to fight a war. They were well armed with weapons, well supplied with clothing and food, and well trained. Their bright red uniforms earned the British soldiers the nicknames "redcoats" and "lobsterbacks." In comparison, the Continental Army was staffed with young, inexperienced soldiers and lacked military leaders with the same knowhow as the British. It was poorly funded and lacked supplies, food, clothing, and weapons.

WAR COMES TO PENNSYLVANIA

By 1777, Philadelphia had become the capital of the Colonies. It was centrally located, and the Continental Congress met there. The British, therefore, felt that the best way to halt the Revolution was to capture the capital city and disrupt the Continental Congress.

General Sir William Howe, Commander-in-Chief of the British Army

On September 11, 1777, the Battle of Brandywine, about 25 miles (40 km) southwest of Philadelphia, became the first major battle of the Revolution fought on Pennsylvania soil. The battle pitted Howe's army of 18,000 men against Washington's army of about 11,000. Washington lost the battle; about 900 American soldiers were killed, compared to 600 British troops. The British entered Philadelphia and took control of the city on September 26, 1777. The Continental Congress fled Philadelphia and met first in Lancaster and then York. For those few days of meetings, each town became in turn the capital of the United States.

On October 4, in an effort to take back Philadelphia, Washington's army battled the British at Germantown. Even though the Continental Army's 11,000 soldiers outnumbered the 9,000-man British Army, the British won. One reason for the victory was that the Continental Army had become confused in the heavy smoke and fog on the battlefield. Many of the colonial soldiers had fired at their own troops.

In the Battle of Germantown, British troops fired on American troops from inside the home of Judge Benjamin Chew. This painting captures the smoke of battle and the feeling of confusion that caused the Patriots to panic and retreat. This defeat put an end to their attempt to retake Philadelphia.

AN EYEWITNESS ACCOUNT

TWENTY-ONE-YEAR-OLD JOSEPH TOWNSEND WAS A QUAKER who lived in the Brandywine area. He recalled meeting the British soldiers just before the decisive battle at Brandywine:

We reached one of the most eligible houses in the town [of Sconnelltown] and soon after divers [several] of the principal [British] officers came in. . . . They were full of their inquiries respecting the rebels [the Continental Army], where they were to be met with, and where Mr. Washington was to be found, &c. . . . The officers aforesaid, were replied to by brother William Townsend, who modestly and spiritedly told them . . . he expected they would meet with General Washington and his forces, who were not far distant, (the front of his army was then in view on the heights of Birmingham meeting house, though three miles [4.8 km] distant from us.)

THE BRITISH IN PHILADELPHIA

Sally Wister was 16 years old when the Revolutionary War began. She lived with her Quaker family in Philadelphia. In 1777, the family fled the city for the countryside just before the British arrived. Between 1777 and 1778 Sally kept a diary that was actually a long letter addressed to her friend Deborah Norris. Below is an accounting of Sally's first experience with the Continental Army:

> *Yesterday, which was the 24th of September, two Virginia officers call'd at our house, and inform'd us that the British Army has cross'd the Schuylkill [River]. . . . Well, thee may be sure we were sufficiently scared; however, the road was very still till evening*

> *About seven o'clock we heard a great noise. . . . A large number of waggons, with about three hundred of the Philadelphia Militia. They begged for drink, and several push'd into the house. . . . They did not offer to take their quarters with us; so, with many blessings, and as many adieus [good-byes], they marched off.*

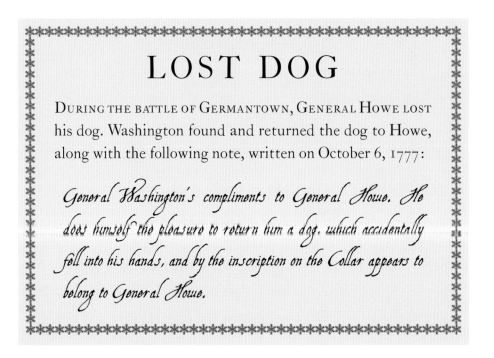

LOST DOG

DURING THE BATTLE OF GERMANTOWN, GENERAL HOWE LOST his dog. Washington found and returned the dog to Howe, along with the following note, written on October 6, 1777:

General Washington's compliments to General Howe. He does himself the pleasure to return him a dog, which accidentally fell into his hands, and by the inscription on the Collar appears to belong to General Howe.

Soldiers in the Continental Army were forced to endure heavy snows and
freezing temperatures on their march to Valley Forge in the winter of 1777.

AN ARMY ON THE BRINK

Dejected and defeated, Washington took his army about
25 miles (40 km) west of Germantown, to Valley Forge.
Here, the army would face one of its greatest challenges—
the winter weather. The soldiers' clothing was worn out,
and they were ill prepared for the snow and cold. Valley
Forge was little more than a grassy hill. Shelters had to be
built and provisions sent for. However, little help came
from the Continental Congress, which was having trouble
raising money.

The soldiers suffered greatly throughout the long, cold winter, and many fell ill, while the British Army stayed warm and well-fed in the homes of Loyalists in Philadelphia. The spirit of the troops can be felt in letters they wrote at Valley Forge. A brigadier general from Connecticut named Jedediah Huntington complained about the camp to his brother, Joshua, yet also expressed his hopes that the conditions would improve:

Loyalists—colonists who remained loyal to England.

> [Cam]p Valley forge 20 Dec. 1777
>
> My Dear Sir,
>
> On the 12th we left White Marsh and crossd the Schuylkill [River] by a Bridge made for the Occasion at Madison's Ford and were all night about it— . . . the Army needs great Repairs I am sorry we have not better Quarters—our Men, our Horses and Carriages are almost worn out with the constant Marches and Fatigues of the Campaign, and there is scarcely a single Convenience about us but Wood and Water—Forage hardly to be got, and Refreshments impossible—but the Army is well disposed and will try to make the best of it—

Ephraim Blaine was the deputy general of purchases at Valley Forge. In his position, he was responsible for buying food for Washington's army. He wrote a letter to Charles Stewart, the commissary general who was responsible for handing out food to the troops:

Camp Valley Forge 16th Feb. 1778

My Dear Sir,

our distresses in camp has been very Great this four days, respecting beef and but very little reliefe yet come to hand. . . . Pork and fish and thirty head of Cattl . . . will afford about two days provisions.

About 3,000 soldiers died at Valley Forge from exposure (being out in the cold, wet weather) and starvation. Despite the harsh weather and demoralizing conditions, the soldiers used the time off from battle to organize and train, most notably with a German soldier named Baron Friedrich von Steuben.

Baron von Steuben, a German captain, drills colonial soldiers at Valley Forge in 1778 in this painting by Edwin Austin Abbey.

Von Steuben had met Benjamin Franklin in France while Franklin was trying to gain French support for the American cause. Von Steuben had fought bravely in Europe's Seven Years' War, but when peace came in 1763 he was unable to find other military employment. Franklin was impressed with the German soldier, who was eager to offer his military experience and services to the Continental Army. George Washington put von Steuben in charge of training the troops at Valley Forge. In a letter dated March 21, 1778, from Valley Forge, von Steuben expressed his excitement at training Washington's army: *"I have met with the most favorable Reception from all the Generals in Your Army, and Gen Washington in particular. His Excellency is willing to Entrust me with the Department of the Exercising and of the Troops."*

During the early days of spring, von Steuben began leading marching drills to instill discipline and unity in the army. He also taught the soldiers the proper and most efficient way to carry their guns and load ammunition. During colonial times, the army who won a battle was typically manned with soldiers who could fire, reload, and return fire faster than its enemy. Von Steuben instructed the soldiers of the Continental Army to practice loading and firing their muskets each time in just eight specific steps. He forced them to practice these steps over and over again until their motions became mechanical. In this way, he was able to turn a group of rag-tag soldiers into a highly efficient army.

General George Washington and the Marquis de Lafayette,
a French soldier who volunteered to fight with the Americans, endure
the cold with the troops at Valley Forge. Lafayette was a loyal and
courageous ally, who helped trap General Cornwallis's troops at
Yorktown, the final battle of the Revolutionary War.

Surviving the brutal winter at Valley Forge would prove to be a turning point for the Continental Army. The French would soon lend their support to turn the tide of the war in favor of the fledgling nation. ✺

CHAPTER EIGHT

A New Nation Is Created

DELEGATES MEET ONCE AGAIN in Philadelphia, this time to discuss a government for their new country.

fter the dreadful winter of 1777–1778, the United States received the news that France had decided to fight alongside the colonists against its old rival, Britain. Once enemies during the French and Indian War, the colonists and the French were now united against Britain.

French military involvement in the Revolutionary War proved to be a turning point in the fight for independence. The French officially recognized the United States of America and promised to send troops and aid to the Americans until the British were defeated. The French

OPPOSITE: George Washington presides over the Constitutional Convention in Philadelphia in 1787.

became the largest provider of military supplies to the Continental Army, and their support significantly raised the dwindling morale of Washington's troops.

As the war continued, the battles moved from Pennsylvania to states in the south. It took more than five years, but the United States finally gained its independence. In 1781, Britain surrendered at the Battle of Yorktown in Virginia. After many months of negotiations, the Treaty of Paris—this time between Britain and the United States of America—was signed on September 3, 1783. (The treaty ending the French and Indian War had also been called the Treaty of Paris.)

The 1783 Treaty of Paris was signed for Britain by David Hartley and for the United States by diplomat and future President of the United States John Adams, diplomat Benjamin Franklin, and ambassador and New York lawyer John Jay.

Philadelphia's role in the founding of the new nation was not yet over. Now that the states were *"in a condition to provide hereafter for their [own] necessities,"* their leaders had to figure out a way to make the new country work. In Philadelphia, the Founders—the leaders who established the United States during this time—gathered to discuss and organize a new form of government for the country.

THE CONSTITUTIONAL CONVENTION

In May 1787, delegates from each state met once again in Philadelphia to make decisions about their new country. The delegates from Pennsylvania included Benjamin Franklin and Gouverneur Morris. At this gathering, known as the Constitutional Convention, the delegates worked together to create a framework for the government. The country faced an economic crisis, and some firm decisions had to be made to control the situation.

The delegates worked all summer, devising a new form of government. They

What Happened to the Penns?

AFTER THE WAR, THE PENNS tried to reestablish their claims in Pennsylvania. The Pennsylvania government paid them for some of their lands, but not all. William Penn's heirs were stripped of 24 of the 29 million acres (9.6 million of the 11.6 million ha) that he had originally received.

The Act for the Gradual
ABOLITION OF SLAVERY

ONE ISSUE THAT CAUSED A DIVISION AMONG THE STATES
during the Constitutional Convention (and which would
not be resolved until the Thirteenth Amendment in 1865)
was slavery. Some states whose economies depended on
slave labor wanted to keep it; others, including
Pennsylvania, wanted slavery abolished. Benjamin
Franklin was a member of the Pennsylvania Society for
Promoting the Abolition of Slavery. In 1780, Pennsylvania
passed the Act for the Gradual Abolition of Slavery, which
provided for the gradual ending of slavery in the state.
Specifically, children born to slaves in Pennsylvania would
no longer be born into slavery, as they were in other states.
They would be free at birth.

all persons, as well Negroes and Mulattoes . . . who shall be
born within this state from and after the passing of this act,
shall not be deemed and considered as servants for life, or
slaves; and . . . all servitude for life, or slavery of children, in
consequence of the slavery of their mothers, in the case of all chil-
dren born within this state, from and after the passing of this
act as aforesaid, shall be, and hereby is utterly taken away,
extinguished and for ever abolished.

threw out the Articles of Confederation—a document that bound the states together during the Revolutionary War— opting to start from scratch. Finally, on September 17, 1787, the U.S. Constitution was formally presented to the delegates who voted unanimously to approve it. They agreed to send the Constitution to the Continental Congress for review. Following is an excerpt from the letter signed by George Washington, that accompanied the Constitution.

In Convention, September 17, 1787.

Sir,

We have now the honor to submit to the consideration of the United States in congress assembled, that Constitution which has appeared to us the most adviseable.

The friends of our country have long seen and desired, that the power of making war, peace, and treaties, that of levying money and regulating commerce, and the correspondent executive and judicial authorities should be fully and effectually vested in the general government of the Union. . . .

It is obviously impracticable in the federal government of these states, to secure all rights of independent sovereignty to each, and yet provide for the interest and safety of all: Individuals entering into society, must give up a share of liberty to preserve the rest. The magnitude of the sacrifice must depend as well on situation and circumstance, as on the object to be obtained. . . .

In all our deliberations on this subject we kept steadily in our view, that which appears to us the greatest interest of every true American, the consolidation of our Union, in which is involved our prosperity, felicity, safety, perhaps our national existence. This important consideration, seriously and deeply impressed on our minds. . . and thus the Constitution, which we now present, is the result of a spirit of amity and of that mutual deference and concession which the peculiarity of our political situation rendered indispensable.

. . . we hope and believe. . .that it may promote the lasting welfare of that country so dear to us all, and secure her freedom and happiness, is our most ardent wish.

With great respect, We have the honor to be, Sir,
Your Excellency's most obedient and humble servants,
George Washington, President
By unanimous Order of the Convention

Before the Constitution could go into effect, it had to be approved by 9 of the 13 states. On December 7, 1787, Delaware became the first state to ratify—formally approve—the Constitution. Pennsylvania was the second, on December 12. The document became the fundamental law of the United States when the ninth state, New Hampshire, ratified it on June 21, 1788.

OPPOSITE: On September 19, 1787, the people of Pennsylvania had their first opportunity to read the full text of the newly drafted Constitution of the United States when it was published in the *Pennsylvania Packet and Daily Advertiser.*

When William Penn first envisioned his land of "sylvan" (forested) beauty, he hoped to establish a colony of tolerance and peace among people who held different religious beliefs. The colony of Pennsylvania had proved to be that and much more. As an English colony, it grew into one of the most prosperous of the thirteen. Its capital city, Philadelphia, housed the Continental Congress and saw the birth of an independent nation. The Keystone State had truly lived up to its name by holding the country together during the American Revolution and the convention that led to the creation of the U.S. Constitution. ✖

The Pennſylvania Packet, *and Daily Advertiſer.*

[Price Four-Pence.] WEDNESDAY, September 19, 1787. [No. 2690.]

WE, the People of the United States, in order to form a more perfect Union, eſtabliſh Juſtice, inſure domeſtic Tranquility, provide for the common Defence, promote the General Welfare, and ſecure the Bleſſings of Liberty to Ourſelves and our Poſterity, do ordain and eſtabliſh this Conſtitution for the United States of America.

ARTICLE I.

Sect. 1. ALL legiſlative powers herein granted ſhall be veſted in a Congreſs of the United States, which ſhall conſiſt of a Senate and Houſe of Repreſentatives.

Sect. 2. The Houſe of Repreſentatives ſhall be compoſed of members choſen every ſecond year by the people of the ſeveral ſtates, and the electors in each ſtate ſhall have the qualifications requiſite for electors of the moſt numerous branch of the ſtate legiſlature.

No perſon ſhall be a repreſentative who ſhall not have attained to the age of twenty-five years, and been ſeven years a citizen of the United States, and who ſhall not, when elected, be an inhabitant of that ſtate in which he ſhall be choſen.

Repreſentatives and direct taxes ſhall be apportioned among the ſeveral ſtates which may be included within this Union, according to their reſpective numbers, which ſhall be determined by adding to the whole number of free perſons, including thoſe bound to ſervice for a term of years, and excluding Indians not taxed, three-fifths of all other perſons. The actual enumeration ſhall be made within three years after the firſt meeting of the Congreſs of the United States, and within every ſubſequent term of ten years, in ſuch manner as they ſhall by law direct. The number of repreſentatives ſhall not exceed one for every thirty thouſand, but each ſtate ſhall have at leaſt one repreſentative; and until ſuch enumeration ſhall be made, the ſtate of New-Hampſhire ſhall be entitled to chuſe three, Maſſachuſetts eight, Rhode-Iſland and Providence Plantations one, Connecticut five, New-York ſix, New-Jerſey four, Pennſylvania eight, Delaware one, Maryland ſix, Virginia ten, North-Carolina five, South-Carolina five, and Georgia three.

When vacancies happen in the repreſentation from any ſtate, the Executive authority thereof ſhall iſſue writs of election to fill ſuch vacancies.

The Houſe of Repreſentatives ſhall chuſe their Speaker and other officers; and ſhall have the ſole power of impeachment.

Sect. 3. The Senate of the United States ſhall be compoſed of two ſenators from each ſtate, choſen by the legiſlature thereof, for ſix years; and each ſenator ſhall have one vote.

Immediately after they ſhall be aſſembled in conſequence of the firſt election, they ſhall be divided as equally as may be into three claſſes. The ſeats of the ſenators of the firſt claſs ſhall be vacated at the expiration of the ſecond year, of the ſecond claſs at the expiration of the fourth year, and of the third claſs at the expiration of the ſixth year, ſo that one-third may be choſen every ſecond year; and if vacancies happen by reſignation, or otherwiſe, during the receſs of the Legiſlature of

TIME LINE

1615 Frenchman Étienne Brulé is the first European to explore what would become Pennsylvania.

1616 Dutch captain Cornelius Hendricksen sails into Delaware Bay and up the Delaware River to the Schuylkill River.

1633 The Dutch establish a trading post on the Schuylkill River.

1638 Swedish colonists sail into Delaware Bay and build settlements along the Delaware River; they call their settlements New Sweden.

1643 Swedish settlers establish New Gothenburg on Tinicum Island, not far from present-day Philadelphia; the governor is Johan Printz.

1644 William Penn is born in England.

1653 Johan Classon Risingh becomes the second governor of New Sweden. He orders the takeover of Fort Kasimier from the Dutch.

1654 The Dutch retaliate and take back Fort Kasimier.

1664 England claims the Dutch lands of New Netherland in North America.

1681 William Penn is granted the lands of Pennsylvania by King Charles II of England; Penn's cousin William Markham arrives in Pennsylvania.

1682 Penn writes his Frame of Government for Pennsylvania; he arrives in Pennsylvania for the first time.

1683 The Original 13 families from Krefeld, Germany, settle the town of Germantown, Pennsylvania.

1688 The first antislavery meeting in Pennsylvania is held in Germantown.

1689 The first school in Pennsylvania is set up in Philadelphia by the Quakers.

1701 William Penn creates Pennsylvania's constitution, called the Charter of Privileges.

1728 Benjamin Franklin buys the *Pennsylvania Gazette* newspaper in Philadelphia and begins his long connection with the city.

1750 Philadelphia becomes the second-most populous of the 13 British colonies.

1753 The Liberty Bell is placed in the bell tower at the State House in Philadelphia.

1754 The Battle of Great Meadows is fought in Pennsylvania; The French and Indian War begins.

1758 The British take over Fort Duquesne (where the city of Pittsburgh now stands) from the French.

1763 The French and Indian War ends with the Treaty of Paris, leaving Britain in control of France's former empire in North America; Pontiac leads Native Americans against the British in the Battle of Bushy Run in Pennsylvania.

1774 The First Continental Congress meets in Philadelphia and sends the Olive Branch Petition to King George III.

1775 April: The Battle of Lexington, the first battle of the Revolutionary War, is fought in Massachusetts.

May: The Second Continental Congress meets in Philadelphia.

1776 June: The Continental Congress meets again in Philadelphia.

July: The Declaration of Independence is adopted in Philadelphia.

1777 The Battle of Brandywine is the first major battle of the Revolutionary War fought in Pennsylvania. The Continental Army spends the winter at Valley Forge, Pennsylvania.

1780 Pennsylvania passes the Act for the Gradual Abolition of Slavery.

1781 The British surrender at the Battle of Yorktown, Virginia.

1783 The Treaty of Paris officially ends the Revolutionary War.

1787 The Constitutional Convention meets in Philadelphia to discuss the formation of a new government; in December, Pennsylvania becomes the second state to ratify the U.S. Constitution.

RESOURCES

BOOKS

*Cohn, Scotti. *Liberty's Children: Stories of Eleven Revolutionary War Children*. Guilford, Conn.: Globe Pequot Press, 2004.

Egger-Bovet, Howard and Marlene Smith-Baranzini. *Brown Paper School USKids History: Book of the American Colonies*. Boston: Little Brown and Company, 1996.

Fradin, Dennis B. *The Pennsylvania Colony*. Chicago: Children's Press, 1988.

Fradin, Denis B. *The Signers*. New York: Walker, 2001.

Hakim, Joy. *A History of US: Making Thirteen Colonies, 1600–1740*. New York: Oxford University Press, 2003.

Johnston, Robert D. *The Making of America*. Washington, D.C.: National Geographic, 2002.

Kalman, Bobbie. *Games from Long Ago*. New York: Crabtree, 1995.

King, David C. *American Kids in History: Colonial Days*. New York: John Wiley, 1998.

Lengyel, Emil. *The Colony of Pennsylvnia*. New York: Franklin Watts, 1974.

Sherrow, Victoria. *The Thirteen Colonies: Pennsylvania*. San Diego: Lucent, 2002.

Swain, Gwenyth. *Freedom Seeker: A Story about William Penn*. Minneapolis: Carolrhoda Books, 2003.

*Wulf, Karin A. *Not All Wives: Women of Colonial Philadelphia*. Ithaca, New York: Cornell University Press, 2000.

*college-level source

WEB SITES

Archiving Early America, Pages from the Past
http://www.earlyamerica.com/earlyamerica/past/past.html
Visit this site to see copies of the *Philadelphia Gazette* and other colonial newspapers. This Web site also has Benjamin Franklin's autobiography online.

The Avalon Project at Yale Law School
http://www.yale.edu/lawweb/avalon/avalon.htm
This site contains the actual wording of laws and acts passed by states throughout the 1700s up to the present, including Pennsylvania's Charter of Privileges.

Doc Heritage: Pennsylvania State Archives
http://www.docheritage.pa.state.us
Easy access to many primary documents, organized according to time periods. Sponsored by the Pennsylvania Historical and Museum Commission.

Explore PA History
http://www.explorepahistory.com
Many wonderful pages that describe the state's history and provide primary documents.

Pennsylvania History
http://www.legis.state.pa.us/WU01/VC/visitor_info/pa_history/pa_history.htm
Sponsored by the Pennsylvania General Assembly, this Web site has detailed information about Pennsylvania's history.

Valley Forge
http://www.nps.gov/vafo
Sponsored by the National Park Service, this Web site has loads of information about Valley Forge.

QUOTE SOURCES

CHAPTER TWO

p.23 "Any government...is tyranny." http://www.explorepahistory.com/Explore PAHistory.do?storyResourceId =42. Original Documents, Excerpts from Frame of Government of Pennsylvania by William Penn, 1682; p.26 "My prison...mortal man." Fradin, Dennis B. *The Pennsylvania Colony*. Chicago: Children's Press, 1988, p.46; p.29 "The Indians...made from corn]. Rivinus, Willis M. *William Penn and the Lenape Indians*. New Hope, Pennsylvania: 1995, p.32; p.30 "The Great Spirit...to do good." Rivinus, p.35; p.32 "these...conditional laws." http://www. explorepahistory.com/Explore PAHistory/storyResources.do?storyResourceId=42. Original Documents, Excerpts from Frame of Government of Pennsylvania by William Penn, 1682; p.33 "governor and...affairs transacted." http://www.explorepahistory.com/Explore PAHistory/storyResources.do?storyResource Id=42. Original Documents, Excerpts from Frame of Government of Pennsylvania by William Penn, 1682; p.33 "a common-wealth...brotherly love." http://www.explore pahistory.com/Explore PAHistory/story Resources.do?storyResourceId=42. Original Documents, Excerpts from Frame of Government of Pennsylvania by William Penn, 1682.

CHAPTER THREE

p.37 "a quiet, godly life...in Europe." Callard, Judith and Germantown Historical Society. *Images of America: Germantown, Mount Airy and Chestnut Hill*. Maine: Acadia Publishing, 2003, p.10; "Es ist...all forest]", p.10; p.39 "From linen...trade alive," Callard and Germantown Historical Society, p.18; p.40 "Book learning...wrack [destroyed.]" Taylor, Bayard. "Pennsylvania Farmer" Excerpted from Earle, Alice Morse. *Child Life in Colonial Days*. Stockbridge, Massachusetts: Berkshire House Publishers, 1899, 1993, p.72; p.42 "This spring...the owls hooted." Schaun, George and Virginia. *Everyday Life in Colonial Pennsylvania*. Greenberry Publications, 1963, p.14; p.45 "Towards the end...Sisters' House. http://www.explorepahistory.com/ExplorePA History/storyResources.do?stwory ResourceId=79. Original Documents, Memoirs of Anna Marie Worbas, nee Schemmel (1722-1795); p.46 "There is a...we stand against it. http://www.german heritage.com/Publications/cronau/cronau4.html. German American Corner: German Achieve-ments in America.

CHAPTER FOUR

p.52 "Just imported...near the Market." http://www.earlyamerica.com/earlyamerica/past/past/.html. Archiving Early America: Pages from the Past, Ben Franklin's *Pennsylvania Gazette*, January 2, 1750; p.53 "I walked up... in Philadelphia. http://www.earlyamerica.com/lives/index.html. Archiving Early America: Lives of Famous Americans: The Autobiography of Benjamin Franklin, chapter 3; p.59 "To the Honourable...So thin plac'd." http:www.docheritage.state.pa.us/documents/lancasterpetitioin.asp. Pennsylvania State Archives: Doc Heritage: Petition for the Establishment of Lancaster County, February 6, 1728/9.

CHAPTER FIVE

p.62 "When the natives...among the Delawares." Rivinus, Willis M. *William Penn and the Lenape Indians*. 1995, p.61; p.62 "was trou-bled...paid for." Rivinus p.60; pp.62-63 "that his children...anything for them." Rivinus, p.61; p.68 "Having made fast...was called Dickewamis." http://www.explorepa history.com/ExplorePAHistory/storyResources.do?storyResourceId=61. Explore PA History: Original Documents: Mary Jemison Describes her Adoption into an Indian Family; p.70 "And whereas great...allow settlement." Rivinus, pp.66-67.

CHAPTER SIX

p.75 "My being many...military purposes." http://www.earlyamerica.com/lives/index.html. Archiving Early America: Lives of Famous Americans: The Autobiography of Benjamin Franklin, Chapter 10; p.76 "A decla-ration from...and fightings." http://www.qhpress.org/quakerpages/qwhp/dec1660.htm. Quaker Heritage Press; p.78 "Since the Men...biding them blush." Griffitts, Hannah. *The female Patriots*, 1768; p.81 "[his] Majesty's...subjects" http://ahp.gatech.edu/olive_branch_1775.html; "to use all...British Empire." http://ahp.gatech.edu/olive_branch_1775.html; pp.82-83 "these United Colonies...totally dissolved." http:www.colonialhall.com/leerh/leerh.php. Colonial Hall: Biographies of Founding Fathers.

CHAPTER SEVEN

p.89 "We reached one...distant from us.) http://www.explorehistory.com/ExplorePAHistory/storyResources.do?storyResourceId=11. Explore PA History: Original Documents: Local Youth Recalls Encounters with British at Brandywine; p.90 "Yesterday, which was... they marched off." *Sally Wister's Journal: A True Narrative*. Bedford, Massachusetts: Applewood Books, 1902; "General Washington's compli-ments...General Howe." http://gwpapers.virginia.edu/education/kids/quest1.html. The Papers of George Washington: Learning About George Washington, Educational Resources; p.92 "[Cam]p Valley forge...best of it—" Boyle, Joseph Lee. *Writings from the Valley Forge Encamp-ment of the Continental Army, December 19, 1777–June 19, 1778*. Bowie, Maryland: Heritage Books, 2000, p.1; p.93 "Camp Valley Forge...two days provisions." Boyle, p.54; p.94 "I have met...of the Troops." Boyle, p.87.

CHAPTER EIGHT

p.99 "in a condition...[own] necessities." http://www.yale.edu/lawweb/avalon/diplomacy/france/fr-1783.htm. The Avalon Project at Yale Law School, excerpted from "Contract between the King and the Thirteen United States of North America, February 25, 1783; p.100 "all persons,...for ever abolished." http://www.yale.edu.lawweb/avalon/states/statutes/pennst01.htm. The Avalon Project at Yale Law School: Pennsylvania: An Act for the Gradual Abolition of Slavery; pp.101–102 "In Convention...of the Convention." http://www.yale.edu/lawweb/avalon/const/translet.htm. The Avalon Project at Yale Law School.

INDEX

ABOUT THE AUTHOR AND CONSULTANT

LISA TRUMBAUER has written more than 30 books for middle-grade readers, including biographies of great Americans Frederick Douglass and Paul Revere. Titles among her other nonfiction work are *Immigration to the United States: German Immigrants and Russian Immigrants.* Trumbauer earned her Bachelor of Science degree in journalism from the University of Maryland. She lives in New Jersey with her husband, Dave, their dog, Blue, and two cats, Cosmo and Cleo.

KARIN WULF is an associate professor of history and American studies at the College of William and Mary in Williamsburg, Virginia. She earned her Ph.D. from Johns Hopkins University and is the author of *Not All Wives: Women of Colonial Philadelphia,* as well as numerous articles on colonial Pennyslvania. Wulf is the book review editor of the *William and Mary Quarterly.* She lives in Rockville, Maryland.

ILLUSTRATION CREDITS

1685

BAFFIN BAY

ARCTIC

NEW NORTH WALES

NEW SOUTH WALES

HUT

Chocakiaby or Nation of Strong Men

Hanston

L. PISCOUTAGAMI

Nadouelian

NEW

Tinthoyha

Isati

The Fall falling of the Lake

LAKE SUPERIOR

North Mountaine

NADOU

Tract of Land full of Wild Bulls

LAKE HURON

ILLINOIS

LAKE ER

NEW MEXICO

NEW ALBION

CALIFORNIA

NEW

Ref Coronado

Pueblo los Reyos

SEA OF CALIFORNIA

NEW MEXICO

MEXICO

MARAT

NEW BISCAIA

THE GOLF or BAY OF MEXICO

ZACATECAS

MEXICO

YUCATAN

SEA

OF

NEW SPAIN

HONDURAS

S. Bartholomew

S. Peters I.